The Year of the Butterfly

☙

by Abigail Mitchell

Write Bloody UK
www.writebloodyuk.co.uk

Copyright © Abigail Mitchell, 2023.

All rights reserved. No part of this book may be used, performed, or reproduced in any manner whatsoever without written permission from the publisher except in the case of brief quotations embodied in critical articles or reviews.

First edition.
ISBN: 978-1-8380332-8-6

Cover Design by Angelo Maneage
Interior Layout by Madison Mae Parker
Edited by Fern Beattie
Proofread by Fern Beattie & Robyn Hill
Author Photo by Emma Marney

Type set in Bergamo.

Write Bloody UK London, UK

Support Independent Presses
writebloodyuk.co.uk

We'll talk of sunshine and of song,
And summer days, when we were young;
Sweet childish days, that were as long
As twenty days are now.
William Wordsworth, *To A Butterfly* (1801)

Love is like a butterfly, a rare and gentle
thing.
Dolly Parton (1974)

The Year of the Butterfly

The Year of the Butterfly

Part I - *rainbow*
MAKE THEM GAY, YOU COWARDS! 15
THE QUEEN OF EVERYTHING 16
PRINCE PHILLIP 17
THE WELL OF LONELINESS 18
REASONS I DON'T WANT TO HAVE SEX WITH YOU... 19
JULY OR BUST 22
COMING OUT IN LITTLE TOKYO 23
THE GARDEN OF THORNS 24

Part II - *casket*
OSLO '22 29
OUR FRIENDSHIP 30
BOXING DAY 31
THE QUEEN OF EVERYTHING (REPRISE) 32
IF WE TALK ABOUT BODIES 33
THE POET OF NEW YORK 37
SECOND STAGE TATTOO 38
SLOW DECAY 40
GRIEF BEFORE GRIEF 42

Part III - *reformation*
THE REASONS I DON'T BELIEVE IN GOD ANYMORE 47
SORROWS 48
ZOMBIE PLAGUE 49
NON-COMPULSORY LOVE SONG 50
GREAT WAVES 52
THROW OUT THE WHOLE DAMN MAN 54
DIAGNOSIS 54
RED FLAGS 56
SHADOWMANCY 57

Part IV - *no paradise for flightless birds*
90028 61
BOUGAINVILLEA 62
PALMERITAS 63
HER, TOO 64
THE FIRST TIME I LOCKED MYSELF IN 65
WE DON'T NEED ANOTHER POEM ABOUT CALIFORNIA ... 67
KINGS GAME 68
BAD ANALOGIES FOR ANXIETY... 69

Part V - *solstice songs*

- AN ODE TO OURSELVES IN 2006 73
- THE CITY OF I LOVE YOU 74
- ESSEX GIRLS 75
- THE SECRET CHORDS 76
- NO, I REGRET ALMOST NOTHING 77
- A SPELL FOR BAD DAYS 78
- IN THE BACK OF THE UBER... 80
- SWEET DREAM LULLABY.. 81

Part VI - *chronophage*

- CONSTANTINA'S BOX 85
- CURSE SCARS 86
- PUCK'S LAMENT 88
- BEFORE I REALISED WE WERE BAD FOR EACH OTHER 90
- LYING NEXT TO YOU 92
- AT LAST 93
- LOVE POEM #19 95
- UNFORGIVEABLE CURSES 96
- BODY ISSUES 98

Part VII - *the year of the butterfly*

- FIRST DATE AT KINGS CROSS 103
- I AM GLAD THAT YOU ARE HAPPY...104
- THE YEAR OF THE BUTTERFLY 105

Part 1

rainbow

MAKE THEM GAY, YOU COWARDS!

Do you remember the first time you saw
Keira Knightley in *Bend it Like Beckham*?
I rewrote the ending in my head, of course
and Jess and Jules grew old together,
scored themselves a couple of kids
and shagged on the pitch at least twice.
In my fanfiction I altered the epilogue,
Hermione explored Pansy Parkinson's chamber of secrets,
Luna got creative with their magic wand
and Ginny already played for my Quidditch team.
Look, I was Team Paris in *Gilmore Girls*
and Team Rosalie in *Twilight,*
which basically means I have a type.
Sailor Neptune's girlfriend is her cousin in England,
which is – not poetic, actually, just fucked up.
Is it too much to ask for a lesbian renaissance?
Where Thelma and Louise drive off into the sunset,
Rizzo helps Sandy out of the catsuit,
Velma shows Daphne her Mystery Machine
and nobody dies in the end?

THE QUEEN OF EVERYTHING
AFTER RYAN BEATTY

God is real –
and she lives here,
in East London.

On the holy day we eat clementines on her sofa,
bare breasts both of us, Belle and Sebastian on the speakers –

When the song changes she punctuates with a kiss,
citrus trails on her chin, collarbone collared in juice and sweat –

and I am beatified in her gaze, electric crackle of belief –
I believe the world should be remade in her image:
B-cups, blue eyes, the birthmark on her shoulder –

the queen of everything on a throne of grasping hands,
greedy mouths.

When the rapture comes she takes my hand:
the stars, the darkness exploding right before us,
sunlight spent on her best blanket.

When she sends me back down again I am not ready for it:
I stumble out into the night, stare into the bus stop pane
at this stranger with wild eyes:

this mortal girl, so far from holy,
in a wrinkled little skirt.

PRINCE PHILLIP

charged in sword-first but still fell victim to the garden of thorns, eyes gouged out. Me, I prick my finger on the spindle of my neighbour's blackberry bush, taste the fruit anyway, autumn stain on my teeth like a grinning vampire in a pink jumper. It's not about courage, if I have any, not serendipity either. All the things I've never known will coalesce here in the same way, the tower of jade without windows or footholds, my hands unfit to climb. There will be a price to pay for everything we have ever loved: the voice or the sight or the coach to a pumpkin at midnight. Me, I'm not afraid of my worst desires. I've seen them – the falling bridge by the old library, the moonlight spilling onto thin pages as they scatter. The river is so dark with its own secrets. The things I would do to cross it are imaginable: a coin in my mouth, or over my eyes, or look how empty these pockets are. I pay in the copper taste as I bite my tongue, don't say the things I'm supposed to say, don't pass go or collect the riches of all of you. The leap is too big and my thighs are still shaking. The sword is too dull, the tower a city block, the fruit too sour for me not to close my eyes. I'm paying the toll anyway because that's how we move forwards: chest of rubies, bloody fingers, the garden of thorns all around. There will be a heavy price for the things I didn't tell you. These promises I swallow; a garden gone barren; a kiss in the corner of my own red mouth.

THE WELL OF LONELINESS

There was a time when we were golden and my
shoulders knew the scent of your hair. I called you love
and my name sat deep in the cavern of your chest;
your teeth learned the shape of it and held
without biting down.

When it rained we'd lie on the floor
to dry our feet at your radiator
and be gentle to each other,
and your eyelashes whispered
into my throat when I took you
to bed and tucked you in against my back.

With the wind in your hair
you could have been a story
I am telling myself, but even I
couldn't imagine something so clichéd.
Even I couldn't steal our time
back from the well of loneliness,
make it tangible again –

if I could,
I'd have given us more of it.

REASONS I DON'T WANT TO HAVE SEX WITH YOU, MAN IN A NIGHTCLUB

Reason one
is that you look like the kind of man
who doesn't wash his own arse
because touching it seems 'too gay',
and I have this thing
where I can tell the milk is going off two days
before anyone else,
so smelling nice really matters to me.

Reason two
is that I only entertain the thought
when I am drunk enough that
consent would fly out of the window;
I don't trust you to know
you should need it.

Reason three
is, okay, if you're amazing
I will still say no, just after hesitating.
I'm medicated, though,
and orgasms are now a marathon,
not a sprint,
and half the time I'm too tired
to cross the finish line.

Reason four;
I know, it's not all about coming, though
you probably wouldn't know
if I didn't. Sweetheart,
sometimes I imagine turning the tables,
sweetheart,
strapping the silicone to my harness
and opening someone up
until you beg for more and – fuck,
I've never said that out loud before –

Reason five:
alright, perhaps I am waiting
for my body to be perfect.
Ignore what you see:
inside me there is the final version,
waiting to be carved out,
the woman with clear skin and ink without holidays and
a liver that can take whiskey
without complaining.

Reason six:
broken clocks are right twice a day
but now is not one of those times.
I've tried it, believe me.
It turns my stomach to remember.
It was December on my grandmother's quilt
and I was frozen there; no way out.
The days after weigh on me
Like he is still on my back,
still telling me to go to my knees,
still biting my own blood into my mouth
so I can't scream…
That is not the point.

Reason seven:
I'll admit. I felt it once.
I met a girl who flipped the switch
and I'm still waiting for her inside my head
(I still say her name when my hand is between my legs).
I still imagine it sometimes,
but these days I want more
than a pipe dream;
someone still on my pillow come morning.

Reason eight:
There are other ways to love,
other intimacies that might be enough
if you gave them a chance, like
the way I used to slow dance with her
in her room; sleeping
curled like matching parentheses,
stroking her hair, her laughing at me
as we cooked over the flames

of the bonfire, her calling my name
as it burned and I didn't even see it,
ashes to ashes to dust
like what became of us and

Reason nine:
If I lay my cards on the table,
perhaps you could actually see:
I am not just just an ace of hearts, to discard,
but a diamond, and a queen.

JULY OR BUST

My nails score lines in the clay as
the wheel keeps on spinning –
strong foundations ruined
by shaky hands

                                          – grey white of ghost-streaked wrists
                                                thickening, Promethean chains –

I remember thinking
if I could make it through July
I could make it through anything,
stacking dreams like Lego bricks
on top of other dreams
to build something unmalleable

                                    – clay eagle kiln-cooked and wingless
                                except, when launched, a projectile in flight –

like someday I want to ride horses
through the ocean with bare thighs
and shave my hair down to its final inch
be the mermaid-cowboy-monstrous thing
that gender cannot touch

                                          – Attic priestesses round amphoras,
                                                    brick and black and white –

I want to claw away the mud,
unearth myself at least
from the sodden mass I call my body
and emerge, no hollow in the centre anymore

                                              – I am no wheel-thrown vessel
                                            for the dreams of old white men! –

so when August comes I am ready
to face it;
to become anew, on purpose

                                                        – like all epics begin

COMING OUT IN LITTLE TOKYO

The first people I gave my truth to kept it safe.
That was why I let them hold it;
spilled into a sake jar and shared around the table,
toasting to the future.
I didn't know that I would
love them, which made me braver:
open enough to lay it on the table and
smooth it beneath my fingers. None of them
hesitated before they scooped it up, deft in chopstick hands
like it was easy. Like it was fine
to be sure of nothing, alien in a foreign town,
gripping my spoon with two hands
and hoping it wouldn't slip through my fingers.

The ramen was pretty good, in the end. Nothing like
I'd ever had. A whole egg floated precarious in the broth
and to my surprise, didn't sink.

THE GARDEN OF THORNS
after Richard Siken

Shut out the last of the light. Feel the way your breath leaves your body. Feel your hand on my shoulder, the warmth, the firm pressure of your fingers pressing into my hip as we dance: like possession, yours and mine and ours, and that grounds me, because home is not the house where we grew our skin. That was temporary. Home is now the sluggish thud of your heart and the way I itch to say come here, look, I'm tangible, look at all the ways I can fill up your empty spaces. There are things you can love and there are the things that must be wild, like dandelions in the grass, or the monster in our blood that tells us to do bad things – as if it's a decision – and I have given you a road map to tell you where to find me. You can't help but follow it, a trail of breadcrumbs into the garden of thorns: a wound and a hearth and the tight cage of your thumbs against my jaw like an apology. I dream about your cold feet on my bare ankle, or the starlight dripping onto thin pages. Think of the bridge over the water by the old library, your blistered fingers, moonlight making claims upon our bodies. We are all dreaming that we belong. Sketching out a life in cautious pencil. Dreaming of a god who made another person to fit us. Dreaming of a tombstone and our names in crumbled cursive. Maybe there is somebody who could love you.

I am dreaming it all for you like maybe this is a fairy tale. Here is the hunger I have to consume you if you'd let me. Sometimes I am afraid of my own desires. There are no words for it; for the way you would taste. Heavy on my tongue, the heaviness of wanting. For how you'd let me in through the narrow gate and say, here is the garden of thorns. Here, I have made this place for you to call home again. But I know how that story ends. I was trying to tell it so that it could be real to me, but there are no words for the language of bodies, the tongue of possession, for the gaps between the trees where the darkness waits. The words are nothing. The forest is nothing. There is nothing to say but to feel the weight of you on my chest when I am alone, as if we were lying on the floor, or six feet under with a stone that says we belonged together.

I am waiting for you to say it. I have drawn the map for you, your hand is on my shoulder, and you are too bright, you are too lovely for me not to let you carve me open, for me not to dream of our garden of thorns – how you might tend to it. We are in the garden of thorns and we are not our desires, and you ask me what I want and yes, I want you.

I hope you might kiss me then. Soft mouth and the careful fit of your hand around my pulse. Perhaps here, in my party dress, you might think we belong together. You, your empty spaces, us, the stone bridge, the steady slide of a slick tongue in the quiet,
saying, yes, please, yes.   But you don't.

Part II

casket

OSLO, 22

Horror is a man with a gun
on the streets that were bursting
with flowers, garlands,
Progress flags hanging from trams
and baby buggies and lovers' hands.
The red stripe of life becomes sullied,
blood blooms through cotton and spandex:
our brothers and sisters and siblings
shivering on the ground
when they should, today,
have been lifted up.

Hatred is a man with a gun
on the streets I first wore the colours,
first marched in joy,
the people with open palms
bent with grief and anger,
grasping for each other.
My friends, out on their balconies with
glitter tracks on their cheeks
spilling to their collarbones
though they should, today
be dancing.

Another year, Oslo, we will be proud again:
hang up the bunting on Karl Johan.
build the cheerful booths at your park
pose for pictures on the Elsker stairs,
write *alt er love* on black and yellow placards.
Dress as Vigeland's lovers in bronze and green,
to show we are still standing
and will not be silenced.

We will overcome this man, this gun,
(tell me that love can survive him).

OUR FRIENDSHIP

Like I am a vending machine for your emotions: an ear to feed your misery into until hope comes out of my mouth, catharsis in your hands.

Like I am a receptacle for your worries, spilling over the brim like a glass too full of water.

Like there is a 'space to let' sign on my shoulder and I am a hollowed out cave for your troubles to make a home in.

Like I have said *look how deep I am! Look at the cup of my chest, and pour yourself into it. Give me more! I can take it!*

Like friendship is a box that you can put your hurt into and I will empty it. I might – but my hands hurt from carrying it with my own burdens. I might – but I didn't know we were doing this today, I left the box at home.

Like you wouldn't ever call me unless you had weights upon your shoulders. Tonight, I thought that we were just two girls in an empty bar drinking California red. Tonight, I thought that you were content to drive down the lanes with me chasing a pink sunset. Tonight, I thought, for just a moment
—

Like if I'm not there in front of you, stitching your organs back in, I don't exist.

Like I am seven feet under with the weight of you on my chest.

I am wondering if I could ever be more than a place to bury your dead.

BOXING DAY

we tested the god of the year and two hands reached back
        to snap the wishbone;
two cars peeled apart at the intersection in the dead of night;
            wild eyes met through windows;
        our family, at the crossroads, splintering ghosts in the back seat
      without music playing.

                that dark night we were
wounded little creatures, we stared into the headlights, said *fuck*.
      i didn't know there were so few quiet places to grieve in.

that night we saw the shroud of what cannot be unseen,
   the hours turning over
            like flipping sand in sturdy glass;
      the traffic light turned green and so we must pass go, collect
   ourselves, the pieces on the
                board still all in play;
i wore her lucky penny around my neck, the sick crack of severance still
   echoing in my
ribcage,
      it was building, building –

           we left her memory on the beige carpet, parted ways,
        drove home for christmas cursing, and
                by twinkling lights we sat wrapped up in grief;

and that night,   in a small house,
    he bent at the waist, a final time,
                            to kiss her papery cheek.

QUEEN OF EVERYTHING (REPRISE)

The truth is that citrus makes my stomach hurt,
acid thinning the lining.
She was not peach-soft, nor golden, more like a
sherbet sting on an ulcer –

She bit so hard my mouth was bruised for days,
the lie blooming under the surface.
I drank through straws 'til the blood drained out,
the *oh* of my lips in some parody of ecstasy, but

losing my faith was inevitable, she said.
The pedestal I built was too tall
for her to stand on, the weight of my
devotion too heavy to carry.

I was naive, before:
my heart on my sleeve, my heart on her floor,
my heart beneath her heavy boots.
I trusted her not to step forwards –

but now she promenades on with her head held high,
queen of pretenders crowned in pyrite
and clementines.

(I think you know I could have loved you, I said, after.
Before my orange-coloured glasses shattered,
you were mine.)

IF WE TALK ABOUT BODIES

X.

I don't remember what I was wearing, but after it happened, I took photographs: the dress was pure white in the frame, an exposed "V" at my neck. In the photos; my skin is deep red against it and the blood is blooming to the surface. I am pale, even for April, like some Victorian maiden unmade in alabaster. I remember that the club lights came up and he pulled back enough for me to push away from the recesses of the DJ booth. I remember that I went home in a cab and took pictures in my bedroom… and sometime after midnight I posted them to Twitter instead of crying. I still don't know why I did that.

X.

Zadie Smith once said that you can tell a young woman, a member of my generation, by the way we talk about bodies. What we talk about when we talk about bodies. She says that she reads, in our stories, the distance between our emotions and our physical forms. How we talk as if dissociated from it: "The body is treated like this strange thing you have to drag around." I'm not my body, but it's a vessel by which I present myself. Like how the stripes and colour of a wild animal show it to be dangerous.

X.

On the other hand, it's not the having of teeth that makes the shark a predator. It's how it uses them – tearing its prey to pieces. My body isn't who I am, but it's a car that I'm driving. So yes, I guess I do believe that my body is something I must carry. Separate from the thing I call my self.

X.

Sometimes I am still the pigtailed girl in the woodlands hiding in the hollow trees, so the dress will be red, and the hood will be red, and I will carry a basket of shadows in case I grow hungry. I see a dark place and I encase myself in it, slip into shadow like it can contain me, but I am ever expanding, the shape of me filling up rooms like smoke. I crawl out on my hands and knees and that's why they're always bruised, green on my skin shining like stained glass ghouls. I have been staring my whole life into the abyss and it has never once looked back. Its eyes elude me, which is why I poke at it like stirring fire, sling my hook down and down and wait for the answering tug.

X.

The pain is not imaginable. I squirmed away from him, wishing it might hurt just the smallest bit less. Each second I believed that I couldn't hold on a second longer. I don't remember if I cried out, if he swallowed those sounds as gladly as everything else.

X.

I think perhaps, these days, I look like a person who might court violence. Might blur the lines between hurt and hurts-so-good. I understand. When you look "alternative" enough, are openly queer enough, people think they can ask you anything. Think you'll know about shibari or where to buy fetish gear in men's sizes. I do know the answers, even, to those questions. I understand because I know how I look now. But before I looked like this – when I was a sweet girl with blonde curls – someone caught me by the throat mid-thrust and didn't think he needed to ask permission. And after, when I had blue hair and a single flower on my arm, someone made me go to my hands and knees and hurt me for an hour without a soft touch to give pleasure. It's been eight years since I have had a touch like that that isn't like facing down a wild animal, feeling it bare its teeth.

X.

"Because critical attitudes towards fat people are so prevalent, some fat people internalize negative societal messages. This can cause fat people or even average weight people who feel fat to place restrictions on important aspects of their lives, such as going to school, changing jobs, buying stylish clothes, dating or enjoying a sexual relationship, or even seeking medical care. Such restriction of activities is also associated with higher levels of depression." - Bacon, Scheltema, and Robinson, 2001.

X.

These days I wear bright colours because I don't want to be afraid. I don't want to show that I am vulnerable. See, I don't believe our bodies have ever been our own. How many years, after all, did I spend building mine in someone else's image? How is it possible, too, to own a thing that you can't keep safe? How can you be a guardian of something if it isn't sacred? If bodies are a temple then ours have all been desecrated. Every altar in pieces. Every woman I know.

X.

We came of age with the stick-thin models of the 2000s, the ana and mia sites, the cult of size zero. We became women with the body positivity movement exploding, unlearned our most formative ideas of beauty in attempts at self-love. We listened to Lizzo songs and accepted we weren't having thigh gaps and we told ourselves again and again that we were beautiful, no matter what they say. The funny part is that I don't believe bodies need to be beautiful anymore. They just need to be ours.

X.

Ground yourself, they tell you. Feel your blood beating in your toes, feel the texture of your skin beneath the pads of your thumbs, and ground yourself. Breathe: in and in and in and in and out until your lungs are clean and beautiful. Listen to the sounds that birds make (and do not imagine that they are taunting you). Listen to the rustle of the cat exploring the kitchen (and know there is no intruder, no brandished knife). They tell you to find something to bring yourself back into the moment, yank you out of your head to notice the chill in the air or the way mint bursts across your tongue when you eat too many breath strips. Imagine you are cutting off the panic at the strings, they say. Imagine. That's not how I imagine it. Grounding, I mean. I know there is ground beneath my feet. See, here is reality, and here I am – uncomfortably tethered. Like Jack handcuffed to the pipe while the Titanic goes under. How I imagine it is that the waves are rising and I don't know how to paddle. The waves are breaking and my lungs are full of water. Here is how I see it: sometimes we sink instead of swim. Like stones into a pond. Like stones inside our bodies. Like –

X.

You cannot possibly imagine how ruined I am for gentleness. I can hear my own pulse at a hand on my shoulder, stomach turning at the one on my knee. When the girl I'm seeing looks me up and down I bite my own mouth at the instinct for flight. When she kisses me I cannot hear the sweet things she says after without brimming over, ants crawling over my body and waking me, gasping, in the night. People say that our generation has a problem with intimacy. Yes. But I don't know what that problem is. Is it giving it too freely or never at all? For me, the answer is both. Emotional and physical have never come hand in hand – and the former I have lost nearly as many times as I have found it. So I push myself until my stomach hurts, watch my peers marry and fall in love like it's normal to shudder at the thought. I couldn't accept her sweetness.

X.

For a long time I have been sad at the way the world is too small to escape sadness, and the same with anger. I am full of it and the world is full of it, which is why we draw these screaming faces on the walls, paint each other red and roll around on the cream carpet. I am off with my head or perhaps just ready to depose, impeach, lead a coup to the front steps of everything that hates me – or I could, except these days it's all I can do to rise from the sofa, shuck the fuzzy blanket and greet the morning. I am so tired and misshapen. Some days I am too small to fill my own body, the air left in a deflated balloon, and I struggle to carry it, the weight of the world on my (not inconsiderable) shoulders. Other days I am bloated with the things I could say, the neverending scream swallowed, gut swollen with bad-feeling. Some of you set the forest on fire and sell the hoses for profit. Fuck you forever. Fuck the horses you rode in on, fuck the fancy armour; we are fighting in secondhand boots and recycled cardboard, and we made the banners ourselves and brought them to your gates with our own rough hands. Fuck you the privilege of not being afraid, not shooting at Goliath with a pile of pebbles, not lying under the duvet and holding the mattress while you shake. The world is ending and you are building bunkers with swimming pools and air conditioning. The world is ending and you are putting on your best suit, blood diamonds and fox fur, dancing on the bones of our planet while we watch on tiny screens.

X.

Of course I remember what I was wearing. The dress still hangs in the back of my closet. I've washed it so often that it's shorter than I would wear, now, faded purple patterns on the white. It's not so angelic. Wide, fluted sleeves, yes – and a neckline low enough to be inviting. I stopped telling people that, for fear of that look on their faces: that comprehension, that moment the story becomes more than black and white. It would be easier to forget, but I still wear it, the white hem above the ink on my thighs. Perhaps, one day, I'll throw the damn dress away, but that's not even the hard part.

X.

Perhaps, my body, I'll do more than drag around.

THE POET OF NEW YORK

we are reading the news again and
we are rolling our eyes back into our heads
to study our insides and
we are wondering if we are as good as we thought we were
because
we are sick of our own company.
i am tired of seeing my own drawn face
on the monitor.
i am alone when i hear that
the poet is dead,
a brooklyn bed and a ventilator,
her sister on her knees.
the poem of her is living anyway,
louder in this chamber i call my body.
chelsea, chelsea –
when she left us the world was so quiet
that the grief rang clear as a knell.
we are all invited to it.
i would not have gone to her funeral
except that nowhere was not her funeral,
and the news was bad, bad everywhere,
and it has been so long since
i had her song first in my hand.
the poet is dead. the poem is still living.
the solitary voice in the abyss rings clear.
the one inside us now is like a litany, a eulogy.
listen to it closely now,
or don't. i don't care.
we are all, she says, going to die here.

SECOND STAGE TATTOO

The marks on my skin felt nothing like needles when they were being made. They only felt permanent after the swelling went down, like

how my favourite band broke up, and five years later I played them after your funeral and finally wept.

How I made myself a bouquet on my own body that wouldn't wilt, and when I showed my nan she said *whatever makes you happy*. The sparrows mean

victory over hardship, apparently, something endured, and the pretty dagger through the heart means willingness to kill.
So I chose something different,

something about willingness to keep on living, walk through this world on my own two feet in the crystallised snow and not slip,

listen to the birds not singing on the fence by the empty bandstand, see the breath in front of my face as proof that I am among them,

that I'm not beneath the covers seeing how slow I can force my heart to beat. Awake, out in the world, these tinny guitar chords in my ears keep me angry,

which is easier than being sad. The ink only burned as she was wiping the blood away, which is typical, she said, and

I did not grit my teeth against the wound as it was made – that was after, when the mark had settled, itch subsided, skin flaked away. When I saw your face on the back of the service card

I finally wept,

and haven't called your name since. See, I know you can't hear it. See, when my favourite band were not my favourite band anymore, I played them anyway,

turned up the volume in my rented flat, danced on the lino in my socks, naked but for the polyester blend and the fresh brand I chose myself, blood and black on white. I imagine, if you heard this, how you would frown at the frigid air, at the music playing, at the petals that burst from my body like needles

and make me angry, which is the second stage of grief.

SLOW DECAY

After the storm passes I am lying in bed and the birds
outside are warbling high and clear. God, they are too shrill in
my ears, god
          -forsaken banshee creatures,
suburban sky. Tonight I am reading a book about
a woman who disappears, and when I flip the last page closed
              there I am
in the lamp-lit mirror, naked, cocooned by my bedclothes
and five-day sick sweat, wondering if only monsters
do monstrous things.
          If it counts if you are doing them
to yourself: picking at scabs with ragged fingernails,
chewing the dry skin from your mouth.
If there is nothing but the smell of VapoRub, menthol in your
nose, and that burn
like you've been underwater for hours,
scoured the copper taste of blood from your bitten cheek.
            I wonder how long it takes a body to atrophy in place.
      A mind to slow its dizzying roll, and slip away.
      I am lying here
and the hours are not passing by.
They say that you should only sleep when it is
dark outside, but that isn't my problem, far from it:

I think that I could listen to the rain for days
and never sleep again.

But
        the storm passes. I feel it, like grieving some loss;
want to rip off the covers, rush outside,
feel wet mud under my toenails and breathe in the moss-green
air. I want the good excuse to run (through the deluge)
and when it thunders, a better one to scream,
        scream,
taste my heart in the back of my throat where it's been
living lately, rising up in me with its butterfly wings.

The birds still singing.
    The clock still ticking.
            The smell of the grass after hours of rain

After it passes I am lying in bed.

I am thinking about vanishing.

(A dumb,
        slow
decay.)

GRIEF BEFORE GRIEF

The summer you were dying
it crested 40 degrees.
The Lionesses won the Euros
and Boris finally handed in the towel,
so the bad news was half-expected
even when it stung like a wasp
tipped from a Coke can into my mouth.
In February you were fine but
by June you were wasted,
a ghost in the shell of your own body,
only your voice the same —

Now it is July and we are waiting
for the call.
The hospice is alright, I think,
for a place that reeks of death.
A saucy old lady takes your sandwich order,
the pretty nurse rubs your feet.
We bring you bright-coloured ice lollies
because ice cream was a small victory
when they finally took out the tube —

I don't know where to begin
to miss you yet. I dream you are
spinning me round the garden,
a small demon in a pink T-shirt,
sausages stuffed in both our pockets
snuck from the kitchen counter.
I wake up with a bitten tongue, now,
mouthful of rotten tomorrows,
fear dripping from them like too-ripe fruit.
Tell me how to grieve you while you still can.
I have arrived too early here
and there is no guide to walk these paths with.

All I want is everything, once more, so
I'll know it's the final time.
Another Christmas in the jumper I bought,

another photo of your cat on her sleeping bag,
another car ride with Mellow Magic on the motorway –
the future has a hole in it exactly your size.

Now it is August and we are waiting at your bedside.
The words don't come, no perfect thing to say.
I am waiting with your hand in my hand,
your tears are filling my eyes.
I am dreaming of you in the doorway, like before,
turning back for a last wave goodbye.

Part III

reformation

THE REASON I DON'T BELIEVE IN GOD ANYMORE

is that I would rather be enlightened than obedient. The original sin was a woman, tempted, tasting that apple of knowledge. I feel that. In my bones I am the same. Today I made a pie of the entire orchard, gorged myself on it, fed on it 'til satisfied I was cast from the garden – the gate of which opened to a new world. Decisions were mine to make, my life a wide open sky. I believe even now: there can be no paradise for flightless birds. I know it because outside of the garden we don't try to return, just build it again and build better, cram the nest with shiny things and let the sacred geometry of our faith hold it up – faith in our own damned selves, faith in the things we learned on the journey out. The ocean cannot wash them away. The cracks in the earth can swallow up everything – not me, I say, because look at these wings. Forget the wax and feathers. I taught myself to soar in the middle blue, clouds on my back, dance of the hawk in golden spirals. From up here the garden is small but the world is more vast than one person could imagine. So ripening and round, the apple of my eyes, the green fruit bursting on my tongue.

SORROWS

"When sorrows come, they come not in single spies, but in battalions."
   - *Hamlet*, Act IV, Scene V

My body
is a territory I cannot
conquer. Barren landscape of
an empire in decline, Ramesses the
Great in an empty desert.
My sorrows are not spies, but battalions
turned to mutiny; the ocean
of rage in me raging, of course, forest
of melancholy blooming in anxious rain.
I am no commander and my
defences are too weak: the
Grand Army runs from Borodino,
fleeing winter, scorching the earth
which is, of course,
still burning.
My body is the kingdom I cannot
reign over, castle sealed shut
by thorny vines. My mind is a
locked room inside which a tiny dictator
rules with a sweaty fist, shouting
ATTACK! ATTACK!
like there is an enemy at my gates
and not cold air and
an empty courtyard; shouting
YOU MAY TAKE OUR LIVES
like the tragic hero and not
Mel Gibson in a kilt. My hands
tremble like they are holding a sword
made of the problems I don't have; my eyes
blur searching for columns beyond the horizon.
I am so tired of fighting, is the thing, but
I'm trapped in this warlike nation.
If it were not treason, I'd put my
head on the chopping block.
OFF WITH HER HEAD! OFF WITH HER HEAD, I SAY!
The tiny dictator has
other plans.

ZOMBIE PLAGUE

After graduation they begin popping up
everywhere. Going down like flies,
the carcass of youth, first line of every
indie girl guitar song. The plague
is fast-acting. First one, then another, then
mortgages and discount gowns and
sonograms, social media shutdowns.
Abundant, the epidemic of life
going unreported except for in my drunk texts,
my best friend's fear of moving away
(though she does it anyway).

Years of nothingness and nobody,
my empty road, flying here and there
and everywhere I look are the walking dead.
This isn't your brother's apocalypse,
tinned food and shotguns.
I think I'd be good at that.
Here the zombies learn to talk
but only in collective pronouns.
We loved that movie, we love our new air fryer,
we think you need to get your shit together.

Do you think during the Black Death
there were people who wondered,
*Hey Death, why don't you
want me?* No boils, no fever,
no septicaemic glands, but
when the town crier came calling them to
bring out your dead, they'd say,
take me, take me, I'm the last one left.

But you're living, he'd say. *But you're free*, he'd say.
You could find a rat and get it over with.
I could find someone and settle is the analogy.
It's a matter of learning how to die to me, you know?
Flatlining youth, my fear of grey furnishings –
But who wants to be the last living on Earth?

NON-COMPULSORY LOVE SONG

We pour one out for the
pretty girls in poems
who beg to be devoured or
to devour, who unhinge
their jaws like great snakes
to swallow the lie whole.
No woman's heart in the wolf, and her:
red lipped, hooded eyes,
riding into the distance.
Pour one out for the women
in their wrinkled sheets
as cocoons, telling themselves
stories as the sweat cools on their bodies.
Coffee cup in hand. Fresh ache warming her thighs.
This morning she woke at dawn to watch the
birds fall from the nest
and never land.
This morning she stood naked as a babe
in his bathroom to stare
herself down in the mirror,
wrote a poem to the stranger in the glass
and let the steam wash it away.
As far as I remember,
the reflection isn't enough.
Sweet girl, I see you. It will all be alright.
Step back from his forest of hands
and choose tenderness. Walk from
his fly-trap mouth and
come lie with me amongst
the daffodils, braid rosebuds
into your silk-spun hair.
In this one you don't have
to surrender anything.
In this one you can keep the
castle of your body warm and lit
and never feel obliged to open the gates.
Walk three times around your bed,
claim your space away from the window.

There are other ways to love,
apart from the language of bodies.
Listen to them sing and close your eyes with me,
imagine it.
The birds all find their way back.

GREAT WAVES

Perhaps there are languages in which
our words aren't overbaked
or failing to rise, or kept in glass jars like
illuminated manuscript under lock and key.
Or: perhaps we shatter the glass
and grant our sisters
lullabies in sacred verse,
which is punk rock,
which is primaeval screams from belly to gullet,
which is spelling out my name
with my hands in the shape of a fist,
open palm, little finger salute.
This will be accessible or it will be bullshit.
This is how we make our rage refined,
sugar cane into granules of
Butler in theory books and Judy Chicago's
dining table laid in museums
with no knives. But anything can be a
weapon if you wield it well enough,
even anger. Suck the blood from your wound
and the poison is all that's left.
Suck the poison out and your kiss becomes
deadly.
Sometimes I don't want to kiss at all.
Keep it, darling, in the corner of your mouth.
Noncompliance is an act, like
THEIR INACTION IS VIOLENCE –
but we don't talk about that.
It doesn't fit neatly into a hashtag,
same way that voices
cannot fit into seashells or Ursula's locket.
Same way that waves have been disproven
but we ride the swell of anger to different crests,
wind in our hair and salt on our tongues,
like perhaps, this time, we'll ride it farther.
Like perhaps, if we sing loud enough,
our songs will reach the shore.

THROW OUT THE WHOLE DAMN MAN

In the roulette of love
my friends have bet their hearts
on red and turned up black,
gambled their bodies to
dealers who won't admit that
the house always wins,
is faithful to itself, its own desires,
and fucks everybody else.

When we were green with our skinned knees and polo shirts
we talked about impossible things,
the colours we would paint our lives,
the food we would serve at our table.
We never anticipated the burden of the game:
the odds stacked against us,
the cheaters and the liars and the
men, hungry for prizes.

It's too long ago to remember what we dreamed of.
Those shiny-lipped girls in their party dresses
are women, now, with ground-down teeth
telling stories about survival.
In the game of hearts we have learned to bet low,
our cards ever closer to our chests.
I have held so many hands, watched so many
cry at losses then keep going, going, going.

But I burned the whole table to the ground.
That's my secret:
when my house of cards tumbled, I never rebuilt.

DIAGNOSIS

Doctor One
says that i should eat less chocolate
and find a boyfriend
which is not a medical diagnosis
and so
it doesn't help. Spoiler alert:
I don't ride into the sunset on a golden dick.

Doctor Two
thinks diazepam will do the trick
but only temporarily
and after that i will be fine because
I am just a 'sensitive young woman'
which is not a medical diagnosis
but I tell him, okay, I'll try it.

Doctor Three
gives me SSRIs
after reading me questions from a printed questionnaire
in a voice that says she couldn't care less
what I answer.
She tallies my points like a maths problem
and writes me a script,
which isn't a diagnosis but is
more than I expected.

I try a therapist after that:
she charges me £70 and tells me to come out
like that will fix everything
and it doesn't.
She tells me I'm too still to be as anxious as I say I am
which isn't a diagnosis
and is, in fact, excruciating.

Doctor Four
is American, pristine,
calm in the back of a Harley Street wellness haven.
I pay £50 for a man(!) who actually listens(!!)
but tells me to up my dosage

and won't give a diagnosis
because he's not a psychiatrist
and apparently that's a "liability issue".

The internet
tells me I am autistic,
have ADHD and
actually, that thing
after sex has a technical term, too,
but the waiting list is two years long
for a fucking diagnosis
and nobody will take you seriously
without one.

Experience tells me
that we are all of us in limbo,
spoonless, we struggle on,
waiting to be seen through this
revolving door of shit.
I give myself the diagnosis
and do the treatment plan myself;
because a woman in pain is a reality,
not a problem,
and nobody else wants to solve it.

RED FLAGS

so hungry that you feel the slip of cold water all the way to your bladder
so tired dizzy you take the stairs on all fours
your throat so dry you can't swallow without retching

waking up, gasping, the ticking in your ears
louder, louder, the clock of your heart
stuttered to wakefulness

the sanctum of your fresh sheets sullied by his back sweat
the mirror under a dirty towel, the windows steamed up,
tape over the webcam,

so gentle-touch-starved that a hand is a brand
in red hot iron:

> *but it's only what you asked for*
> *and you opened the gates to the keep yourself*
> *and you waved him over the drawbridge,*
> *right?*

(and now the scrap raised over the parapet
is stained so bloody
they'll say it's not white).

SHADOWMANCY

I used to wish I could unpick
    the seam from body to shadow
        or cut the threads at my feet
            with tiny scissors and not bleed.

I didn't want to see the dark shape
    of me lengthening, unfurling,
        willed into being under torchlight
            like a rabid creature caged –
                and me along with it.
Sometimes we cast two shadows:
    we sit to tea with our demons,
        surround ourselves with their secrets.
Your shadow and mine have sat at bars,
    watched us dancing under flashing lights,
        toasted to survival as the bass dropped because
            they knew we could never outrun them.
I was glad of it,
    the formless sense they made
                together.
Sometimes, small, sometimes vast,
    too dark to note their beginning and end.
I still think of the darkness we built for each other
            but it's time to let it all go.
Send it down the river
    to the place where the light runs out.
        I will wait – ready to forgive you everything.
Blood, sweat, and suture.
    Scissors in hand.
                (Stitches in silk black thread.)

Part IV

no paradise for flightless birds

90028

The day I moved north
it was *one-oh-seven* Fahrenheit.
My English brain couldn't translate it
but my body could,
climbing the hill towards the one-oh-one
dripping sweat to sizzle on the pavement.
The elevator was broken,
the freezer our only solace;
we bought two boxes of popsicles
at the 7-Eleven on Cahuenga
and counted how long
twenty poles took to melt.

We carried my life up a flight of stairs
in less than an hour and
when I blinked I was alone.
I lay on the hardwood floor
beside a tower fan,
wet flannel on my face
like a poor man's air conditioning;
I flung the balcony doors open
to the sounds of the freeway;
smelled the weed from the underpass as smoke
drifted through the balustrade.

That first night in the barrio was disgusting
and still everything seemed possible.
An empty space to start over,
a chance to rise up from the dust.

BOUGAINVILLAEA

I thought I heard a voice in the bougainvillaea bush this morning.
I was eating a donut three days after it was good,
but it was good enough for breakfast:
stale dough, raspberry jam, lemon glaze. My fingertips
were the kind of sticky that seems impossible to unstick
and the sugar-sweet air was bright with 10 a.m.
I was sitting in the wicker chair as the gardener sprayed his hose
as if the drought was a far-off memory,
A bare chest, bare head, as if
the sun wasn't peering insidiously over the veranda
ready to roast, prickling my skin in warning like
I could burn you alive
and keep burning. The voice,
it said *go, run, as far away as possible* but
I am contrary and did the opposite,
pink flowers blooming around me in my pyjama shorts,
 as I shrank down, stuck, stayed put for you –

bewildered as I was
in the oppressive blaze of paradise.

PALMERITAS

Did you know that in Spain, actual Spain, they make biscuits like palm leaves from folds of puff pastry? I say *biscuits* but you know what I mean, America. I say *Spain* but their origin is French and I ate them in Catalunya. Sometimes they are called *pigs ears*, and the Mexicans call them *orejas*, and in Puerto Rico they top them with honey! Anyway, when I see a palm tree, California, this is what I imagine: the abuelas in L'Escala at their countertops, pressing soft dough and butter into layers with their hands, folding, slicing thin; an echo of how it feels to see dark lines of tree trunk on blue-orange sky; or how the voices in my knees tremble, as if to say *sit, feast on this,* gorge, land of dreams in laminated dough; watch it come back up again as the American nightmare on postcards, Saturday cartoons, Lucky Charms you eat until your belly hurts. When I see your palm tree, California, it's like my life folds down, compresses into inches: by which I mean this incendiary moment.

(By which I mean I'm in the oven, about to flake into pieces.)

HER, TOO

When she says the word
it's like gobstones
rolling out of her mouth,
or that bit
where Ron is vomiting
slugs onto the grass.
We smooth it out onto our laps
and look at it a while,
grotesque.
What happened? I ask,
and she looks at me like
that isn't the question –
but she answers,
because

it's like popcorn kernels
stuck between her teeth, and rotting,
though she picks at them
with ragged fingernails;
because
it is festering globs of
rancid meat,
too tough to
swallow,
though her jaws
work and work,
until

what happened? I ask,
and it chokes her, she retches.
I hit her in the back
and then
she spits him out,
half-chewed.

THE FIRST TIME I LOCKED MYSELF IN

there was no yellow wallpaper   those days
I didn't listen to the bricks   singing
my Art Deco apartment   arches
of cream-painted frowns   chorus
of get out, get out   until   at last
   I did

the bathtub was cavernous,   acoustic,
   though I could not hum along
I did not relax in the water   each slam
of the balcony door   gunshots?
intruders in the sanctum   despite
   my brain saying otherwise

worse was the red air   the haze
of drought-filled days   the smell
of gasoline, stale piss-soaked   Mary-Jane
   on the freeway hill
perhaps they explain the things   I wrote
   big and bold across a page
to take up space and   onwards
onto my hands and knees and   spilling
   over to the bulb-lit mirror
the roach-cleared sink and tiny   dead flies
I had so much space to think   taunting
me, the   spareness
   like   an invitation to start over

I filled the rooms with music when   I could
   and when I couldn't
     I stuck photos to the walls
and peeled the paint from them with tape   I thought
the cabin fever was bad enough   the seas
were unimaginable, I couldn't bear   to look
   at the waves
they were lapping against the windows

there was   an art to being alone   back then
I have forgotten how to make it   paint it

when my hands are less steady   no way
   to hold on anymore,

my voice cut at the   chords
              nowhere   to run
now no mouse-holes   in which
      I can slip through   the cracks
      to see the sky again
wild and pink as the fever in   my bones
and listen to the dawn   singing hello

WE DON'T NEED ANOTHER POEM ABOUT CALIFORNIA,

city of dust, dust of solitude, undisturbed
by rain in seven months
(*fuck you California drought!*)
with its stars all neon bright white light
or carved into the pavements
or lying in a bathtub while a
cockroach scuttles up the side;
we don't need another small town girl
in a downtown bar drinking five-dollar Schlitz
slurring about how she didn't get the job
(*the only jobs left are hand, rim, and blow!*)
with mascara on her t-shirt
from crying in the bathroom
when her gag reflex kicked in
over and over and over and over and
we don't need another road to California,
or from California, road trip songs or
cheap motels, hotels,
(because *fuck you, Eagles songs!*)
and we don't need another
sweeping anthem of swelling guitars
and sweat, sweat everywhere, no
more dirt beneath our toenails, no
puking under the exit
where the 101 hits Hollywood,
all pale-faced-dehydration-dance-club
half-dead, our rancid hope
because *we were promised more than this,*
more than palm trees and insects and
the ragged fingernails of the man on the Metro train
who grabs us by the wrist,
because we are afraid to shout, we are
afraid to call our moms on payphones
or 3 a.m. drunk in dive bars and tell them what's up,
we are afraid to stop,
to say *fuck you California!*
and afraid we can't go home.

KINGS GAME

the man in the next seat is drinking vodka
    with a twist of lemon and
  he keeps putting his hand
      on my shoulder to tell me about his
    daughter, light of all lights, his darling sweet
    princess, & he says she is
 my age
 and will never leave him
   like his wife did and
she doesn't
understand hockey
       like I do. but of course
all I want
is to drink my beer in
     peace,
  watch the captain wrap the puck around
for a hatty,
      four rows from the glass,
  & of course
 all I want is to stumble
safe into the night, high on winning, become
      one with the sea of men
 in red sweaters – who will never
linger on my breasts
like hungry dogs
      or jeer at the girls shovelling ice
or tell me I can't
   like hockey; who will
  not wolf-whistle or
 shout *fuck you, lady* in parking lots, who
won't ask where my boyfriend is
      or try to explain the icing call; who
won't crowd us in with their big shoulders
    at the concourse bar to breathe
their nacho breath on our faces as the intermission's
          ending,
never satisfied with our answers,
 whispering
sweetheart, baby, bitch –

BAD ANALOGIES FOR ANXIETY THAT YOU THINK ABOUT WHEN YOUR FLIGHT HAS BEEN DELAYED FOR EIGHT HOURS WITH NO EXPLANATION, THANKS A LOT, DELTA

Diazepam is how it feels to run through viscous syrup with
a large man chasing you. He has calloused hands that
make you shiver when he touches you, like when his
coarse fingers brush your elbow on the backstroke.
You are running through a field of molasses which
is of course not never-ending, but of course your
legs are getting tired because they're spindly and
inadequate. Hey, syrup is hard to run through.
The man has large thighs and you would be
into that, maybe, if he wasn't screaming.
If you cover your ears, it's like it's not
happening. Don't look back. No! That's
a dumb idea! Look: the thing is, you
could leave the syrup field any time
and run out to the lane by the tall
grass. The thing is, you chose
the syrup to slow him down,
but you're tired of it anyway.
The thing is, at any point
you could emerge: feel
cool air on your thighs
for a moment,
at last!
Free!

('Til he catches you.)

Part V

solstice songs

AN ODE TO OURSELVES IN 2006

We wrote it sitting on the bathroom sink,
in our own sweat and salt and sticky from the floor,
scrawled kohl on our own arms to wash away come midnight.
Love letters were mixes with sharpied plastic cases and
sideways smiley faces, well before emojis,
before front facing cameras;
crowded together in the park for the timer on the swings,
crouching out of frame until the flash went and our
knees wobbled and we crashed to the ground in our ripped jeans
laughing.

He made a song of our bodies and we sang it all the time,
drove out to listen
in his car without heating, lashings of rain on the roof,
the night we stood dripping by the fire escape and danced ourselves dry to
images of night skies, hungry wolves, and mountains on the horizon.
The bass line was the steady tattoo of
never getting out alive, we couldn't imagine it,
soaring guitar of birds with broken wings that fall
from grey sky to grey pavement.

We were screaming along with him when we first heard what our
voices sounded like in our own ears, the
G note of our will to live, the echo of the cry
of a baby in its tenth second of living. The thrill of it,
bright and shiny like silver glitter smeared on eyelids with our
fingertips as the small god of electric dreamers blessed our dingy church.

When the chords of hallelujah rose up from the pit
it was morning on the other side.
Our ears are still ringing.
Our veins still full of life.

THE CITY OF I LOVE YOU

I have been dreaming about the finale that we didn't have but might. Our lives before the sun set on the city of possibility. Anything that could happen there will happen if we let it, because anything that has happened can happen again: our glasses full of deep red, we spill onto your mattress laughing. Tonight we are a carousel full of moonlight. Fucking hell, I've missed you. Yes, it would have been fantastic. All these years I have missed your mouth, dreamed of glitter in your hair, chasing each other on your messy bed, the slow ballads on the docks. There is music playing here, too: street accordions, wild pipes. In the city of I miss you we are briefly giddy, spinning around like we did before, champagne-made lighter than the cold air. Our feet remember the steps and our shoulders the frame, waltzing marionettes with no strings attached. In the city of I love you we will dance anyway. It could have been this easy. I want to be lit up and I won't stop saying it: sweetheart, my candle, my low flame of steadfastness. Christmas fir in my belly with the lights burning bright. Take me to church in the room where you've been living. Two decades, one breath, our past unravels. Let me excavate it, here under your pillow where the bottle rolls. I know, I'm sorry, you've never known what I wanted. I am wiser now, so I can tell you if you'll hear it: In the city of tomorrow I want my friend to kiss my throat, I want your hands, your pure heart, this one kind night to sit with my worse decisions. I want to know what I could have wanted before all the fucked up things. No more what ifs for me. It would be illuminating. I need you, my friend, to take me by the hand, to lead me down the paths we never took. Take me to tomorrow and then leave me at the other side, watch the sun come up from rooftops, buy me fresh coffee and sweet buns. There will be a lock on the door this time and the window will be winter bright. In the morning we will tear sugar to pieces, answer the questions we never asked. Teach me what it's like and I won't ask again. My dearest friend, my almost lover. Take me to the city of no regrets.

ESSEX GIRLS

They say the soil under Colchester is
russet-soaked with Boudicca's name
in her enemies' blood
but her ghost is still screaming.

In Manningtree the bones of Anne West
and one-legged Liz Clark lie uneasy,
the Witchfinder's rictus grin
looms from the town sign.

Barking Abbey is a school, these days,
its abbesses now stories
like Wulfhilda running through sewers
to escape a man's obsession.

Perhaps in time their stories will be told:
how Alice Perrers became the Wife of Bath
and Mildred Cooke advised her golden queen
and the goat woman of the Bower had a sanctuary
and Henria Williams wore purple, white, and green
(as she stood her ground and marched and, starving, screamed)

but still the Essex soil soaks up their names
as Mother takes her girls back to her loam;
and on the coastal winds our voices soar
the estuary carrying our souls.

We were the shortest days, the darkest nights –
the pendulum unbalanced, braced to swing.
It was war paint on our faces, all this time:
crimson slashes painting hungry mouths,
as our mother's mothers called us
for their reckoning.

THE SECRET CHORD

If love is like music then mine is a record ender,
the last song played at a party when
your sleeves are rolled up and sweaty.
My love is *Wonderwall*, *Closing Time*, and
New York New York with the feet kicking up in the air.
BAH da-da-da-da, et cetera, et cetera.
I'll sing the words so loud that you wouldn't
call it singing, exactly, solo and coda,
Taylor Swift and the Black Parade
in the next breath.
At that point the night is over.
You'll take what you get and what you'll get is me:
eyeliner pooling in my salty eyeballs,
kissing your nose in the taxi and
falling asleep.

If love is like music then yours is Newton Faulkner:
weird and earnest and understated.
(No offence.)
You played *The Book of Love* cross-legged
on our staircase, slow and steady and
sweet on ukelele.
I can hide in the in between of it, sneak in under
your bright voice and the buzz of your fingers on strings
til you realise I'm harmonising –
but that's okay. The song's made for it.

If love is like music then ours is the secret chord.
Hallelujah. You taught me how it goes.

NO, I REGRET ALMOST NOTHING

but at night i still hear the crickets
chittering through screened windows

the saltwater tang of ocean lingers,
warm gulps of air scattered in a small room
by a tower fan sputtering dust

some things slip through our fingers like sand,
others mud, others like birds released from cages
only to spiral back, peck out your sad eyes

me, i want to rid myself of all the bad things,
shrug off the mantle of them from my shoulders
and keep the good safe in locked boxes,

jewels of my life strung up by golden chains
that won't tarnish, glittering
like the opal on the horizon.

at night, i hear the future play your lullaby on a Spanish guitar.
she cradles you in her leathered hands.
the waves carry you away.

A SPELL FOR BAD DAYS

step one:
make a crown from glue and paper
like we used to: mum's hand
steadying you in dungarees.
babes, she says, the first step is to let it dry,
and the next is not to pull it over your eyes,
circlet of thorns like a shirt made of hair.

step two:
don't punish yourself, okay?
we are all trying to pretend that
what happened never happened,
bind it up in the book of mistakes and
let the spine catch fire.

step three:
you are cleansed by the smoke and ashes.
here is your encyclopaedia of survivable losses.
here is that thing you buried deep,
anchored yourself 'til you cut the cord.
here is your shadow sewn back to your ankles
with whittled bone for needle.
here is the paper rose that lived so long
you doused it in water to watch it wilt.

step four:
one day your body will be mud
for the river or the garden, but
today is not that day.
today you must keep going.
pull up your skirts and scale the wall.
i am waiting on the other side, hand
outstretched, ready to take the baton
and keep walking.

step five:
now tear up the pages
where you thought you didn't matter,
paste another strip onto the mould.
when it dries you will wear your crown
again. *baby, darling, incandescent child.*

step six:
no matter how bad it is, remember, repeat after me:
tomorrow, tomorrow, tomorrow
will be something else entirely.

IN THE BACK OF THE UBER

My feet have salted every borough
with sweat and left no mark:
like kisses on the neck of a fickle lover or
bruises on a fighter gone by morning.
Sometimes I have not cherished
the streets that grew me,
but others, drunk, I cross from west to east
in the back of a fast car.
I tour the sites of my own history and
they have not awaited my homecoming.
Some remain; some are rubble, some evade me
with fresh paint over the old
as we hurtle past in the dark.

I make my vigils pressed to a cloudy window
fingers smudging prints as if, like spectres,
they could pass through to touch empty air:
the park where we span in circles under a big tree to ring in the year;
the station steps of Aldgate, our unexpected refuge;
the bridge between two worlds; the salt beef bagels,
the poetry cafe from our first date.

If I were a tourist I would say *this was the life she lived;*
here are the roads she walked and the constellations
she couldn't see through the smog.
I will try to hold the map in my sleepy hands,
scribble the notes in the margins and hope they won't be erased.

City of my nine lives reborn, streets of my past selves in the dead of night:
let me light a candle to you in my heart before sunrise.
Let me look at you in the dark as we drive away.

SWEET DREAM LULLABY

Sometimes when the day is fading and the birds are flocking to the tree and the blackness of the night is fathomlessly here, I hear it. Darkness is not a blanket. Night is not a warmth. Night is now and here I am sitting on the train, with the push and pull and rattle of the beast beneath my feet, where I ride half-sleeping, cold toes, frigid fingers. Sometimes when we pull up at my stop I feel this tug at me, the moons in my chest, saying: stay aboard, plant your feet into this floor and let it grow you out to the coastline, to Southend with its muddy beach and muddier waters, stay. Imagine you are there to plant your hands into the brownness. Bury your troubles beneath the water. I hear it say: come now. Come, follow this thread with your nose, let the tides caress your soft hair, submerge. Sweet girl. (This isn't ideation.) The sea might feel like freedom. Like darkness isn't a blanket, but deeper, an ocean instead of a sky. Sweetheart. Back in the world a bird is singing. Back in the world I am getting off the train, doors sighing shut as I climb the steps to the street. Home. I'm so sorry, sweet girl. There will never be as much star as there is darkness. (I am learning that.) But sweetheart, listen: you are unravelling it in your sleep, this spool of thread of wound up loneliness in the blanket that isn't the night. Sweet girl. Stay. Submerge. This darkness. (It says.) Come, now.

Part VI

chronophage

CONSTANTINA'S BOX

I am thinking about the sarcophagus of Constantina
and cherubs and vines carved into red porphyry
and a girl whose body is put inside a box and never held again;
about how graves used to come with bells for the risen to pull
and the Chinese would bury in cool sheets of jade
(to keep the soul from demons!)
I am thinking about an Irish wake and the way grief tastes like whiskey
when it burns your throat;
how they pulled a lost king from a Leicester car park
though his hair was blond
and his spine was twisted
to prove Shakespeare wrong.

>I am thinking about all the ways you are alive in me,
>how your brother calls with my favourite hoodie,
>warm from your parents' dryer.
>The DVD in my laptop, the beer bottles,
>empty and brown on my table.

>>(I am remembering that first winter, how I asked
>>if I could keep you. How you laughed,
>>how you said sure! You can
>>put me in the attic
>>with your other decorations; you can
>>put me in a wooden box,
>>treasure me,
>>like the one with the spinning dancer,
>>with the lullaby
>>that will not stop playing
>>though of course the springs are broken.)

CURSE SCARS

Ten years later,
I didn't feel your curse snap
out of place. I'd been working on it,
month after month of picking
at the edges. The sutures
sank into my skin and left no mark,
the threads frayed, then
even the scar tissue stopped
catching my eye in mirrors.

Ten years later I do the dishes
in soapy water and stare at
the middle distance,
remember the north wind
in the kirkhouse, the torrents
of rain, the dress with all the
polka dots. Thank you for
the weeks we slept like
knives there, too afraid to
curl into each other,
for the boosts you gave me up to the roof
to listen to birds and talk about God.

Thank you for asking
me not to kiss you, which made it
all I thought about.
For the first time in my life.
For the love letters that were not
love letters but said the same,
sold me the world, said
I was good when I needed to hear it.
It's not your fault that you couldn't love me.
I know that now.

I don't remember learning it
but it let me unravel you
thread by thread,
piece by meticulous piece,
tapestry of the field of the cloth of
golden days. I remember
how beautiful it was,
and I'm sorry I never told you that.

It kept me warm for years, the blanket
I made of the ache of missing you.

I don't remember it lessening.

PUCK'S LAMENT

it started that night that you caught him
                laughing at a joke you made.
full mouth curving upwards, the jester,
                        pink lips and pale skin.
     his hand, running
                    over the burr of buzzed hair
        cropped close enough for friction.

sometimes when you meet somebody so electric
the world could burn down around you.
                you consider *hello* but find it wanting.
    you consider your voice
                        but it sticks like tar in your throat.

you consider the ghouls crawling grinning from
                your wallpaper:
    you shed the coat your mother gave you
              and the jumper with the fraying cuffs and

  you run
     (with all of the other snapped-off puzzle pieces
                who never learned to fit anywhere)

because
    real and new and potentially terrifying
   are not dark   and nothing   and yes.
       the grasp of a t-shirt in a clammy fist and the moon shining

down on you, barefoot in the mud.
         you are dancing with your limbs, but no deeper

   and, still: that mouth.
              him: smiling in the firelight.

you can't be afraid of the things you want,
                                          only of someday losing them.
you will shake off the debris, scrape the dirt from under your fingernails.
and, then:

    when you are done being a wild thing,
                                you might trade him your smile
for his name.

BEFORE I REALISED WE WERE BAD FOR EACH OTHER

I wanted to tell you that I could be your sanctuary.
Wanted to say *open your sea-green eyes* and slice open your chest
    and wrap your heart in silver ribbons –
        and I will find a safe place for your agonies to flourish.

I wanted to say
    look, I wrote the sky for you.
        Drew eternity onto a coffee house napkin.
    Mapped constellations over your shoulder blade with my tongue
        to taste you and skin and the salty rain.

I wanted to tell you
    all the ways you can wrap yourself
        up in another person:
    in ink and in hopes and in soft blankets by the fire.

I wanted to tell you
    I could be your beacon.
    Guide you home, to your thumb pressing red marks into my hip,
        and the easy quiet of our companionship.
    Through the nights you thrash in thunder and ice
        I would whisper
you down from the tempest.

Some nights your laughter is so bright that I wonder:
    maybe it's you who are the lighthouse.

You tell me
    one day, this ship will just be wreckage.
        The clouds could dance together into darkness
and I'll have forgotten how to be the stars, or the sun, or the moon
        and the safe ways through deep waters.

I wanted to tell you
    to come back to me, *trust me,* but
        I can't shield our soft hearts from the monsters
    we've created.

They lurk under the surface with sharp teeth
    and I'm not ready
      to be devoured.

LYING NEXT TO YOU

& you are lying next to me, how a door stands against its frame: an inch of space between us except for the places we touch, where you might pull me in, or push away, swing back and forth in fear or something scarier. Right now you are still. Your palm lingers on my cheek but you are not listing forward like you want to, not asking me open with your tongue or the uncalloused pads of your fingertips. It's just you and me and the silence of a room with fresh paint on walls, the susurration of your breath before you say it.

I have not said it but I am ready to say it & I maybe do not love you the way that normal people love each other & perhaps I do not need you the way you'd like us to need each other. But I sometimes think about that scene in Dawson's Creek, where Pacey holds Joey's wrist to his cheek and tells her *I remember everything*, and I know that I Pacey love you. Like that feeling when I opened the envelope from Cambridge and I saw the word *congratulations* and how my parents cried in August when I got the confirmation; I Cambridge love you, I August love you, I life-changingly, joyfully, academically love you:

My body is an open doorway and I am waiting for you to know it. It is just you and me, and your eyes tracking across my sunburned cheeks, the press of your thumb under my bones, & we are lying here and I love you: the up and down of your chest under your pyjamas, I love you. You are lying next to me and I lying next to you love you. Say it. I am ready to say it. Lying next to me, lying next to you.

AT LAST

for a second there is something shocking about
       the way she is looking at you,
the gasp that reverberates through
       to your breastbone, the way it cracks you
  open to your core
             (with her guileless sweetness).
you have never been understood before
     and now seems a bad time to begin:
  Etta James on the radio, and her,
     snoring at your back.
but she stays.   together, you
     try again to swim against the current.
           you try again and
  you will remember to breathe this time. your mantlepiece
will be a home: to all of the
          tiny masterpieces that
      the ocean should have washed away, but didn't.
you'll breathe into her hair for the remembered
     taste of salt and joy and exhaustion,
as you sink down tangled together, on a rug
            by the open fire.
at last.
    she will say it, and you will
grip her sweaty palm to you, tighter,
   pressing the crescents of your fingernails – like
          ownership – into her arm.
it's hard, because
  you didn't know that this was what you were waiting for:
the slow and steady way she
     traces your eyelashes with her thumb.
  the timbre of her sighs.
the ocean: singing softly as you float,
       or drift,
      or drown.

for a second there is something shocking about
         the way she is looking at you:
    the soothing press of her fingers against your
ragged edges.

             the way she prises you open, gently,
cautious of what it is like to be vulnerable.
             she is.   and at last, you are understood;
Etta James on the radio, and
       her – sleeping by your side.

LOVE POEM #19

you are inside my skin like a parasite
or the ache
from a really hard fucking

which means

    my body is not a temple
    or has been
    desecrated

UNFORGIVABLE CURSES

There are things I have done that I never learned to live with,
though I flayed myself open for them too many times
and couldn't patch the holes again
and never found the promised absolution at the bottom of
a highball glass or in your rolled up filter paper
or in any god you believed in.
None of that made me forgivable in my own eyes:
no matter how many guts I let fester on the floor
as they trickled out of me or
how hard I tried to punish myself
by not trying to die
when it was always on my shoulder,
an oasis in a desert for the crawling hag
with dust in her eyes.

I can be flat out on solid ground with the half-hazed stars above
to remind me there are bigger things,
but nothing seems bigger than the ways that I have failed
or the people I have hurt
and the houses I have blown down
with three little huffs and puffs to prove that I could.
I swear I wanted to let you in, but I didn't know
how to touch without you slipping through my fingers,
me pulling you into the quicksand that is the only way
I love. I swear,
there are things that I have done that would make you sick
if I could remember enough to tell you, if i could speak
without hacking up a perfect clot in the shape of my lungs,
if I could undecompose them, unbury them, unring the bell
and watch them all come out, to hear the low rumble of guilt
as it rises from the grave with its yesterday rotting, heart torn clean out.

If I could excise the person who did those things I would
pick up the knife myself, but I am living with them instead, I am
sitting to tea with my demons, I am
watching them manifest in the shape of
my own eyes, my own mouth, my holy resurrected sins
in a kitchen sink confessional.
I don't know how you could forgive me.

Please –

I don't know if I want you to.

BODY ISSUES

My body is disgusting.
My body is unloveable.
My body is the thing I fear the most.
My body is too round and too scarred.
My body doesn't fit in airplane seats.
My body doesn't look good in jeans.
My body is creaking at the joints already.
My body is the last thing I look at before I fall asleep.
My body is a monstrosity waiting to happen.
My body is every nightmare I ever had.
My body is not a temple, or it has been desecrated.
My body is a dark room with a flickering light.
My body is a white sheet fortress between two chairs
or a gothic church with a goblin swinging from the spire.
My body is an empty heath, a voiceless cry...
(My body is fucking terrifying, actually.
The thing I haunt when I'm feeling spooky.)
My body is the cave, the well, the lily pond with no bottom.
My body is the motel room in the B-movie we're watching.
My body is a body of open water, rippling in a storm's high breeze.
My body is all the liminal spaces – especially airport bathrooms.
My body is all the things I can bear to believe at a time.
My body is the longest poem I never know how to write.
My body is a butterfly field where joy grows as golden wheat.
My body is a resilient motherfucker, actually.
My body is warm when it's cold outside.
My body doesn't bruise easily, my body is unpeachlike.
My body is a different fruit but it is juicy and ripe.
My body is an advertisement for the queer glory inside.
My body is a glitter bomb ready to detonate.
My body is tall enough to ride this ride.
My body is my body is my own damn body.
(I like my body when it's not by your side).

Part VII

The year of the butterfly

FIRST DATE AT KINGS CROSS

deep in the city   a birdcage made of light
neon and metal   you are under it
you!   standing by the swing
through the deluge   i am translucent
a skeleton of   paper straws

your perfume   i want to stick my nose in
the dip beneath your ear   test how soft the skin is
warm and sweet as peaches   rolled in your hands
i would like to taste them   i would like to come
inside   from the rain   you
to rest your cheek   rest against my heart
hear the rabbit pound of it   beating, beating
take a bite of your mouth   the first time
maybe   meet your eyes again
dare i touch   shorn hair
with holy reverence   holy holy

deep in the city   here   we are together
i am here   love   i am wanting
short hair   peach soft   rainbow of the night

I AM GLAD THAT YOU ARE HAPPY

I was in my room that last summer,
unpacking a year into corners
it didn't fit in,
piling new baggage onto old dust.

We didn't live together anymore,
which meant no more run-ins in the kitchen, no more
passive aggressive missives, carved into butter
with a wooden knife.

In our second-year house
I dyed my hair red in our bathroom,
while you read my poems to another girl
and then fucked her –

I was putting my life into new boxes when you called.
I picked up
on the third ring
so I wouldn't seem eager,

lined everything up on the closet floor,
your apology on speaker,
and tried to put us away,
a car crash wrapped in caution tape.

It took me all these years to see
that you were unhappy,
and not just trying to torture me.

I am in my old room again, this summer,
when you finally cut the tape off.
It tumbles out afresh, a mess,
the question I never asked –

but you are telling me you are happy, at last,
so I delete the words once I've typed them out.
My closet is long empty these days
and I swear
I am happy (you are happy) now.

THE YEAR OF THE BUTTERFLY: A LYRIC ESSAY
after William Wordsworth

i.

When Spring came we hopped into an SUV and drove north into the mountains; it was hot for March; we stopped for water at a wooden lodge and I poured it down the red of my neck. That night we stripped down to our swimsuits, popped a cork in the tub, and toasted each other, steam silhouetted against the hills. My cheeks were sunblushed so my head was light from card games, edibles, and the bluest sky I'd ever seen. We wore short sleeves at midnight, built a fire, flames licking air as my skin prickled in the breeze. The next morning I awoke to fresh coffee on the back deck and breathed in gulps of lake air like pure elation.

ii.

In a kinder world I might be lying in a clawfoot tub beside a wall of glass: verdant greens, pale sky all around. Mug on the wooden table full of tea and honey, bills paid, no tension in my neck.

In a kinder world I might be humming a love song and tracing my fingers through the bubbles after sunrise, body sore from walking in the brisk dawn or tender from a lover's touch. My arms pink beneath the water, pebble as I shampoo my hair.

In a kinder world this morning I would not have read the news before I left my bed, or it would have been a balm. The planet would be in safe hands and we wouldn't have to bear more than we could carry.

In a kinder world I could scrub it all away.

iii.

I've been writing the same line over and over. About stones sinking through bodies. *Life is alternately, inside you, stone or star*, Rilke says. For me life's no more than a garden of thorns. We're all making our way through this labyrinth, wading through mud with pens as swords, cutting through the branches; princes fighting through brambles in red capes. I think we're all trying to unravel ourselves. To free ourselves from the tangle to see the sky, the way that stars look without all the smog. This is freedom. But the truth is that we can't always see the roses through the thorns. The mud is thick, and sometimes we sink, instead of soar.

iv.

I am yearning for her.

The river that flows and ebbs. I sit with her in this wooden shell, learning how to move in time so that each stroke feels like a haiku in calligraphy. In the morning the world is silent but for the birds and the catch of the blade in the water, the steady breaths of the girl I love, the creaking motions back and forth as we row past the meadows. We slip through the water like butter through knives, winds whipping our hair around our faces. Past the cows on the common and the little dogs being led along the muddy path, we soar, past the daffodils growing wild and the blossoming trees on the banks. Lean back, tap down, rock forward, slide up. Catch, push, pull, finish. Again. And again. And again.

v.

I've heard that in the future, life will be very beautiful.

There will be a thousand paths for people to stray from, freedom to forge new ways through old weeds. I say we are already walking the roads our parents never traveled. Our grandparents' maps guide us, but we are marking a new route, carving our names into trees that bend to let us pass. I believe that tomorrow is already here and happiness is not a future tense. I don't need to hope for the future because I am here in it, watching beautiful people do beautiful things. A man is writing the most beautiful song. A woman builds the most beautiful bridge from impossible to real and then crosses it. Somewhere somebody is laughing in the passenger seat of an old car on their way to nowhere, is dressing up in fishnets or pearls or both, is telling somebody else their truth for the first time and being taken by the hand: I love you, I love you, I love you.

vi.

I've been thinking about it, anyway. When the year of the butterfly ends we will emerge, cautious, padding from the door in socks and slippers. We'll peek around the frame, pink-cheeked and golden, then step into the world. No, we can't be young again. Of course not. But we can be reborn; we can shave our heads and paint our faces and burst through the surface for air. We'll drink sweet wine at the dockside bars, shuffle heel and toe on sticky dancefloors, sing, sing, sing together on train platforms and in football stands and in church pews. A stranger will meet your eyes on the street and you'll see their smile. Can you imagine it?

When the year of the butterfly ends it will be Spring again at last.

We will bloom together, turning our faces to the sun, and I will finally take you by the hand.

*A*CKNOWLEDGEMENTS

"PRINCE PHILLIP" and "THE GARDEN OF THORNS" were first published by *coffin bell*.
"THE CITY OF I LOVE YOU" was first published by *Sapphic Writers* zine.
"SWEET DREAM LULLABY" was first published by *pidgeonholes*.
"THE QUEEN OF EVERYTHING" is after Thomas Beatty's "God is Real".
"THE GARDEN OF THORNS" is after Richard Siken's "Snow and Dirty Rain".
The title of "THE WELL OF LONELINESS" comes from Radclyffe Hall's book of the same name.
"Forget the wax and feathers" in "THE REASON I DON'T BELIEVE IN GOD ANYMORE" quotes Stanley Kubrick's musings on the Icarus myth, from his 1997 acceptance speech after winning the D.W. Griffith Award for lifetime achievement at the Director's Guild of America Awards.
"OSLO, 22" is dedicated to the victims of the mass shooting in Oslo, Norway, on June 25th, 2022.
"THE POET OF NEW YORK" is dedicated to the memory of Zoe Mungin, who died of Covid-19.
"BOXING DAY" is dedicated to Dolly Tame; "SECOND STAGE TATTOO" to Terry Mitchell; and "GRIEF BEFORE GRIEF" to Simon Mitchell.

All of my love and gratitude:

To Emma, my soul sister, for keeping me sane enough this year to see this through. To Dawn, my old pal, for the impromptu recording sessions in the forest and in dark alleyways. To Mum, Dad, and Alex, for supporting me in my obsessions even when you think I'm being particularly uncool. To the Johnsons for cheering me on, and to Grandad, for still calling me your little princess. To Sophie and Becki, for all of the prosecco and love when times got hard. To Georgia, for telling me this could never be "too Taylor Swift". To Frankie, Anoushka, and Sapna, for coming to watch me perform in Brick Lane, and to the lovely people at the Sappho Events poetry nights for your repeatedly warm welcomes. To Meredith and the Speak Easy poets in East Ham, for the encouragement and the gratifying snaps. To my fellow postgraduate Humanities researchers at

Southampton, for the support and memes, and to the 2022 Creative Writing students for hyping me up on Zoom open mics. To Ryan Taylor for introducing me to the lyric essay, which quickly became my favourite thing. To my other fellow graduates of the MPW at USC, who were there when I published my first poem, and to my first ever creative writing community, at Peterhouse, helmed by Pete Wilkes.

My sweet uncle, Simon, passed away in August 2022, during the writing of this collection, after a short battle with a horribly aggressive form of cancer. Though he would never have read it, his loss shaped this book in an undeniable way. Simon, I miss you so much.

My nan, Jean Mitchell, passed away in January 2023, while I was editing this book. Nan, I love you to the moon and back.

Thank you a million times to Fern and the Write Bloody UK team for welcoming me into the fold on a cold night in Canning Town. A big shout out to Derrick Brown and Cristin O'Keefe Aptowicz for selling me their books all the way back in 2014 and introducing me to what became my favourite press. Thank you to Sappho and to John Keats and to Mary Oliver – it goes without saying.

Thank you to My Chemical Romance for reforming when I needed you the most; to Taylor Swift for unapologetically making songs about her real relationships; and to the first, second, and third girls who broke my heart, for kindly disappearing from my life so I could write about you without fear.

This collection is for everyone out there who doesn't know where they're going (but knows, at least, that it's forwards). Same, babes. Same.

About the Author

Abigail Mitchell is a writer and postgraduate researcher at the University of Southampton, where she works on queer fabulation and the history of the 17th-century Essex witch trials. She also holds an MA in History from the University of Cambridge and an MPW from the University of Southern California. Abigail's poetry, short stories, and creative nonfiction have appeared in *The Butter*, *coffin bell*, and other literary magazines. You can find her haunting open mics and coffee shops in East London, or on twitter as @hextorian

IF YOU LIKE ABIGAIL MITCHELL, ABBIE LIKES...

The Cardboard Sublime by Oliver Sedano Jones

Ping! by Iain Whiteley

Drive Here and Devastate Me by Megan Falley

The Year of No Mistakes by Cristin O'Keefe Aptowicz

Pansy by Andrea Gibson

Bloody beautiful poetry books.

Write Bloody UK is an independent poetry publisher passionate about bringing the voices of UK poets to the masses.
Trailing after Write Bloody Publishing (US) and
Write Bloody North (Canada), we are committed to handling the creation, distribution and marketing of our authors; binding their words in beautiful, velvety-to-the-touch books and touring loudly with them through UK cities.
Support independent authors, artists, and presses.
Want to know more about Write Bloody UK books, authors, and events?

Join our mailing list at
www.writebloodyuk.co.uk

www.ingramcontent.com/pod-product-compliance
Lightning Source LLC
Chambersburg PA
CBHW022115090426
42743CB00008B/864